666 Horror Creative Writing Prompts

By Walter Blake Knoblock

Copyright 2023

How to use this book: Go to a random page. Read the four prompts. Pick the one you find most interesting. Use it as a launching pad. Some of the prompts are direct, and some are quite open-ended. There are more than 666 prompts in this book, but only for safety reasons.

The old mirror shows your reflection, but not your true self.

A group of friends go on a camping trip in the
woods, only to discover they're not alone.

In a small town, a supernatural entity seems
to be causing chaos and destruction.

The abandoned house on the hill seems to be watching you.

The streetlights start to flicker and go out one by
one as you walk down the deserted road.

You find a door in your basement that wasn't
there before, and it leads to a secret room.

Voices whisper in the wind, warning of a fate worse than death.

A family moves into a new house, only to discover it's
built on top of a Native American burial ground.

You see the same person or creature in all your dreams, and it's not a pleasant presence.

You hear strange whispering in your ear when you're alone, but no one's there.

A strange mist descends on a small town, and no one can leave.

Fear consumed them as they realized they were trapped in a never-ending maze.

A black cat crosses the path of a traveler,
signaling a terrible omen to come.

A group of friends visit a remote island, but soon realize that
they're not alone and that the island has its own secrets.

A group of friends go on a road trip, but soon realize that
they're being followed by something malevolent.

A scientific experiment with interdimensional travel
goes wrong, leading to a group of humans being
trapped in a nightmarish, alternate dimension.

Beware the strange object that follows you
home, it's alive and hungry.

In a post-apocalyptic world, a group of survivors
discovers a mysterious substance that can grow into
any food. But the substance has a dangerous secret.

A young girl discovers that she has the power to control the
elements, but she's not the only one with special abilities.

A woman starts seeing a mysterious figure in her photographs,
but when she investigates, she discovers a dark secret.

A group of friends go on a camping trip, but soon realize that they've stumbled upon a mysterious laboratory.

A group of friends spend the night in a supposedly haunted house, but they soon realize that it's more than just a rumor.

A man discovers an old chest buried in his backyard, but soon realizes that it's cursed.

A mysterious disease starts spreading across the world, turning people into mindless zombies.

A woman inherits an old mirror from her grandmother, but soon realizes that it's a portal to another dimension.

The end of the world is near, and only a chosen few can stop it.

A group of teenagers play with an Ouija board, inadvertently summoning a malevolent spirit.

You see a ghostly figure sitting in the back of an empty theater.

The clown statue in your child's room
moves on its own at night.

A group of space travelers discover a derelict
spaceship carrying a dangerous, sentient virus that
threatens to spread across the universe.

In a remote village, a strange illness is spreading,
and the locals believe it's caused by a curse.

Kneeling before the altar, a cultist summons
an ancient deity to do their bidding.

You see a ghostly figure standing at the foot of your bed.

Shadows dance on the walls of the abandoned mansion, but who – or what – is casting them?

Insects that were once harmless have grown to gigantic proportions and are now terrorizing the city.

A small community is plagued by a series of mysterious disappearances, and the only clue is a strange mist that seems to follow the victims.

You hear a loud banging on your front door, but
no one's there when you answer it.

A scientist creates a new type of AI, but it
starts to become too human-like.

You see a reflection of yourself in a mirror, but your
reflection is doing something you're not.

In the attic, you find a journal with your name on
it, and it's been writing about you for years.

Violent storms rage through the abandoned city,
as if nature itself is trying to destroy it.

Hidden beneath the town square was an
ancient sacrificial chamber.

You hear a knock on the door, but when
you answer, no one is there.

The sound of someone sobbing echoed through the empty
hallway, as I made my way to the abandoned apartment.
Inside, I found a young girl sitting in the corner, her tears
turning into solid diamonds as they hit the ground.

You hear the sound of someone scratching
at your bedroom door.

A small town is haunted by a ghostly apparition
that seems to be seeking revenge.

On a planet where the environment is toxic to humans, a small
community discovers a horrifying secret about their ancestors.

A group of friends explore an abandoned hospital,
but soon realize that they're not alone.

A group of survivors must band together to
escape a city overrun by the undead.

You hear a voice whispering your name,
but there's no one else in the

You see a ghostly apparition of a loved one who has passed away.

A woman starts experiencing strange visions, and soon
realizes that they're all connected to a dark past.

As a couple forge fake papers to escape, they are haunted by the ghost of a previous escapee who was caught and executed.

A group of colonists on a distant planet must confront their own beliefs when they discover evidence of an ancient religion.

The smell of burnt toast filled the room, as I walked into the kitchen to find a figure made entirely of flames standing before me. It spoke in a language I couldn't understand, before disappearing into thin air.

Opening the closet, they found a portal to another dimension.

A woman is trapped in a room with no way out, and soon realizes that she's not alone in there.

You wake up in a body that's not your own, with no memory of how you got there.

You wake up to find a mysterious message written on your bedroom wall.

You wake up to find yourself in a world that's not quite like the one you remember.

Eclipsed by darkness, the town is consumed
by a relentless wave of terror.

You find a cursed mirror that seems to reflect your worst fears.

You hear the sound of someone breathing heavily behind you.

Blood-curdling screams echo through the abandoned
mansion at night, frightening even the bravest of souls.

The old tree in the park has been standing there
for centuries, watching and waiting.

A sentient AI takes control of a space station, trapping
its crew and threatening their survival.

You hear the sound of someone breathing in the darkness.

A man starts hearing strange whispers in his ear, and
soon realizes that something is trying to possess him.

X-rays reveal a shocking discovery hidden
within the walls of an old hospital.

You hear a baby's laughter coming from the
empty room, but there's no one there.

You find a cursed mask that seems to change its
expression every time you look at it.

Knives are found buried in the backyard,
leading to a gruesome discovery.

In a world where all food is synthetic, a group
of rebels discover a hidden farm that grows real
food. But the farm has a dark history.

A group of friends decide to spend the night in a supposedly
haunted graveyard, but they soon realize that they're not alone.

After escaping from a religious cult, a woman must
face the reality of life outside the group's walls.

Whispers of an ancient curse are heard among
the ruins of a forgotten city.

Beware of the old mirror, for it shows
more than just a reflection.

22

You hear the sound of someone singing a
haunting melody in the distance.

When the fog rolled in, they realized they were
not in their own world anymore.

Paranormal activity escalates in the old hotel,
as the spirits of the past refuse to rest.

X-rays revealed something unsettling within the patient's body.

The farm-to-table restaurant boasted fresh ingredients, but their secret sauce was made with something that wasn't quite from this world.

A catastrophic event on a space station leads to the emergence of a deadly, hive-minded entity.

Beneath the old bridge lies a dark secret that no one dares to speak of.

A group of survivors must fight against a virus that
turns people into monstrous creatures.

Obsessed with power, a mad dictator unleashes
a deadly virus on the world.

A strange mist descends upon the town,
and people start disappearing.

A woman starts experiencing strange dreams about a
mysterious figure, but soon realizes that the figure is real.

You hear the sound of a child's music box playing
in the attic, but there's no one up there.

In a small town, a group of survivors must fend off an invasion
of giant insects that seem to be controlled by a hive mind.

A man discovers a mysterious door in his basement,
but soon realizes that opening it was a mistake.

Killer clowns are on the loose, stalking their
victims in the dead of night.

A group of friends go camping in the
woods, but they're not alone.

A man finds a strange journal in an antique shop,
and as he reads it, he realizes that it's cursed.

The coffee shop had a cult following for their signature espresso
blend, but the beans came from a plantation with a dark past.

A small community is plagued by a series of strange deaths, and
the only clue is a mysterious cult that seems to be involved.

A man starts experiencing strange body changes, and soon realizes that he's becoming something inhuman.

A group of astronauts on a long mission must rely on their hydroponic garden to sustain them. But they soon realize the garden has a deadly secret.

Quivering with fear, a group of friends enters the abandoned mine, unaware of the horrors that await them.

A group of survivors must navigate a world where reality itself is constantly shifting.

A man discovers an old diary hidden in his attic, but soon realizes that it's written in a language that no one can decipher.

Xenophobia consumes a small town as they become increasingly suspicious of outsiders.

A group of friends decide to explore an abandoned asylum, but they soon realize that they're not alone.

A group of survivors must navigate a world where the laws of physics no longer apply.

A group of teenagers stumble upon an old book that grants them incredible powers, but at a terrible cost.

A group of explorers discover a hidden prehistoric laboratory where experiments were conducted on humans and animals, resulting in terrifying hybrids.

A forgotten curse had resurfaced, and it was wreaking havoc on the small town.

The blood moon rises, awakening ancient evils that have long been dormant.

You wake up to find a mysterious message written
in blood on your bedroom window.

The upscale steakhouse had a reputation for
serving the finest cuts of meat, but the diners didn't
know where the meat was sourced from.

In a future world where genetic modification is the
norm, a genetic experiment creates a monstrous
creature that threatens to destroy everything.

The jam made from wild berries tasted heavenly, but the
hiker who picked them disappeared without a trace.

Living in a Soviet country, you learn that everything
you say and do is being watched.

A group of students go on a field trip to a supposedly
haunted house, but things start to go terribly wrong.

You wake up to find a trail of blood leading
to your bedroom door.

A young girl discovers a mysterious book in the attic,
only to realize too late that it's a cursed artifact.

The bright blue sky outside turned a sickly shade of
green, and the birds stopped singing. Then, a swarm
of gigantic, carnivorous insects descended upon
the town, their pincers clicking hungrily.

Every dish at the new bakery was a feast for the senses, but the
bakers themselves were rumored to have an insatiable hunger.

A tribe of prehistoric humans discovers an ancient alien artifact
that gives them incredible powers, but at a deadly cost.

The music box in the attic plays a tune that
will never leave your mind.

A team of explorers discovers a cave system that leads to an underground city inhabited by prehistoric humans, but they soon realize that they are not alone.

The abandoned church still echoes with the prayers of the damned.

In a future where religion is used as a tool of oppression, a young woman must choose between her faith and her freedom.

The Italian restaurant's pasta dishes were made with a unique sauce that was only available to select customers.

The carnival rides continue to move even when no one is there.

A group of outcasts must band together to survive
in a world where religion is the law.

Long-forgotten memories resurface in the abandoned
mental hospital, driving those who enter mad.

You see a mysterious figure in the fog that
disappears when you get closer.

A time-travel experiment goes wrong, trapping a group of humans in a future world overrun by dangerous technology.

A group of strangers wake up in a mysterious facility with no memory of how they got there.

A group of survivors must navigate a world where the dead come back to life, but they soon realize that the zombies are evolving.

A group of astronauts crash-land on a planet inhabited by intelligent prehistoric apes who see them as a threat to their way of life.

You see a ghostly figure standing in the
shadows of an abandoned building.

Eerie noises can be heard coming from the old, dilapidated
mansion on the hill, but nobody has lived there for years.

In a distant future, a plant-based diet has become
the norm. But when a new meat substitute is
introduced, it has a terrifying secret ingredient.

In a society where religion is used as a means of control,
a group of rebels fights for their right to free thought.

After being banished from his religious community, a man discovers a new world with a completely different set of beliefs.

Quiet whispers echo through the abandoned church, drawing you closer to the truth.

You wake up to find a stranger sleeping next to you, but they're not human.

Drenched in blood, the abandoned house on the hill beckons you to enter.

A small town is terrorized by a mysterious creature
that seems to be made of shadows.

A team of scientists creates a food additive that enhances
taste buds. But it has an unexpected side effect on the brain.

The discovery of a parallel world threatens to shatter
the foundation of a highly religious society.

Blood-curdling screams echo through the halls of an
abandoned hotel that was thought to be empty for years.

A man discovers an old film reel in his attic, but
soon realizes that the footage is cursed.

After being cryogenically frozen for centuries, a group
of humans awaken to a nightmarish new world.

In a universe where religion is outlawed, a group of
scientists discovers evidence of a higher power.

Locked in a room, a survivor fights for their
life against a relentless monster.

A young couple moves into a new neighborhood, only to discover that all the residents are part of a sinister cult.

A crew on a deep space exploration mission discovers a derelict ship with a dangerous, parasitic organism onboard.

You wake up to find yourself in a different world, with no idea how you got there.

The wine that flowed freely at the dinner party was laced with a hallucinogen that led to the guests' darkest fears.

A woman starts experiencing strange changes in her senses, and soon realizes that she's not alone in her own body.

I watched in horror as my reflection in the mirror began to smile, its teeth elongating into razor-sharp fangs. Then, it lunged forward and pulled me into the glass, trapping me in a world of twisted mirrors.

Just beyond the tree line, a mysterious portal leads to another world.

A small community is plagued by a series of bizarre animal attacks, and the only clue is a strange set of footprints left behind.

You find a strange object in your closet that seems to be alive.

You see a ghostly figure standing in the corner
of your room, watching you.

You hear the sound of a music box playing in
the distance, but it's getting closer.

You wake up to find yourself in a coffin, and
you don't know how you got there.

A woman starts hearing strange noises coming from the walls of her apartment, only to discover it's being haunted by a malevolent entity.

As a man travels to a remote village in search of his missing brother, he soon realizes that the villagers are hiding a dark secret.

A scientist discovers a way to travel back in time to observe prehistoric humans, but their interference in the timeline leads to disastrous consequences.

The smell of burnt hair filled the air, as I walked into the abandoned laboratory. Inside, I found a group of scientists huddled around a machine, their bodies fused together in a twisted, inhuman form.

Knowledge of an ancient ritual is the only way
to defeat the evil that haunts the town.

A family moves into a new house, only to find
that it's haunted by the previous owners.

You wake up to find a strange tattoo on your
body that you don't remember getting.

You hear the sound of a baby crying in the
night, but you don't have a baby.

The abandoned school still has the laughter
of the children who disappeared.

You wake up to find a dark figure standing
at the foot of your bed.

A small town is plagued by a series of strange disappearances,
and the only clue is a strange symbol left at each crime scene.

The dollhouse in the attic is an exact replica of your
home, but with dark secrets hidden inside.

A small town is terrorized by a group of children
who seem to be possessed by something evil.

Unseen forces begin to torment a family who have
recently moved into their dream home.

Strange occurrences in the abandoned school
point to a malevolent presence.

A group of scientists discover a strange virus, but
soon realize that it's more than just a virus.

You wake up to find a stranger in your bed who
claims to know everything about you.

You're never alone in the forest, even when you think you are.

The ghost in the photograph has been watching you for years.

A small town is plagued by a mysterious
fog that seems to be alive.

Eerie laughter can be heard coming from
the abandoned carnival at night.

You find a cursed ring that seems to bring
out the worst in people.

A small town is plagued by a series of unexplainable deaths,
and the only clue is a strange mark left on each victim.

A woman wakes up in a strange place with no memory of
how she got there, and soon realizes she's not alone.

The doll in the antique store window has eyes that follow you.

You find a mysterious object that seems to be calling out to you.

The fast food joint's burgers were the epitome of convenience, but they had a tendency to move on their own.

A group of survivors must fight against a new type of fungus that infects and controls human hosts.

You wake up to find a strange object embedded in your skin.

A group of astronauts on a mission to explore the galaxy discover a planet where religion is the foundation of society.

You wake up to find a strange object
embedded in your bedroom wall.

A man starts hearing strange voices in his head, and
soon realizes that he's not alone in his own mind.

A woman inherits an old dollhouse from her grandmother, but soon realizes that the dolls inside are alive.

A woman inherits a strange artifact from her grandmother, but soon realizes that it has the power to summon a demon.

A group of friends stumble upon a mysterious town, but soon realize that they can't leave.

A group of friends discover an old Ouija board, but soon realize that they've awakened something sinister.

Rats scurry in the darkness of the old subway
tunnels, but what else lurks in the shadows?

On a planet where humans have been genetically
engineered to be perfect, a group of rebels discover
a sinister plot to control their minds.

A group of scientists discover a way to travel back in
time and alter the course of history, but they soon realize
that changing the past has dire consequences.

A woman starts experiencing strange side
effects after taking a new medication, and soon
realizes that it's not just a coincidence.

As a group of friends visit a haunted mansion, they soon realize that the ghosts are not the only things that are dangerous there.

You see a ghostly figure standing in the middle of a dark forest.

Misty tendrils of fog drift through the abandoned
town, concealing a sinister presence.

In a society where the government controls every aspect
of citizens' lives, a resistance movement discovers
a sinister, mind-controlling technology.

A group of scientists discover a new virus that turns
people into bloodthirsty monsters, but soon realize
it may be too late to stop the outbreak.

You feel a cold breath on the back of your
neck, but you're alone in the room.

A group of teenagers visit an abandoned amusement
park, only to discover it's haunted by the ghosts
of the park's former employees.

The painting you inherited from your aunt seems
to change every time you look at it.

You feel something crawling under your skin,
and it's not just your imagination.

Visions of a bloody past plague the minds of
those who dare to enter the old castle.

Cryptic symbols etched into the walls of an
abandoned mansion hold a dark secret.

A research team on a remote planet discovers that the native
plants have taken on sinister, carnivorous characteristics.

Obsessed with the occult, a mad scientist conducts forbidden experiments in his basement.

As a group of friends go on a hiking trip, they soon realize that the forest is not what it seems, and that they're not alone.

The antique watch you inherited from your grandfather stops at the same time every night.

In a universe where religion is outlawed, a group of rebels fights to preserve their beliefs.

You wake up to find a strange creature
sitting at the end of your bed.

You see strange shadows moving in the
dark that shouldn't be there.

A family goes on a road trip, only to find themselves trapped
in a town that seems to be stuck in a never-ending time loop.

As a strange mist descends on their town, a group of survivors
must figure out what's causing it and how to stop it.

In a small town, a cult has taken over the government.

You find a cursed book that seems to be
changing every time you read it.

Darkness descends upon a small village in the forest
and nobody who ventures in ever comes back out.

A man starts experiencing strange blackouts, and soon
realizes that he's committing horrific crimes during them.

A tribe of prehistoric humans discover an abandoned alien spaceship and the technology within causes them to become obsessed with power and domination.

Every night, a mysterious figure watches from the shadows, waiting for its next victim.

A group of friends go on a cruise, but soon realize that they're on a ship of the damned.

In a world where religion is forbidden, a group of rebels discovers a hidden underground society where it is still practiced.

The abandoned hospital still echoes with
the screams of the patients.

A family makes their escape attempt through the forest,
but soon realize they are being hunted by a supernatural
entity that preys on those who try to leave.

Zombified creatures roam the abandoned city,
seeking out fresh victims to devour.

You see a ghostly figure walking down the street
that disappears when you approach.

In the darkness of the night, the statue in the
park moves when no one is looking.

A group of survivors must fight against a new breed of
monsters that are unlike anything they've ever seen before.

You hear strange, muffled sounds coming
from under your bed at night.

You feel like someone is following you, but
when you turn around, no one's there.

Quicksand traps a group of hikers in a desolate
canyon, where they encounter an ancient evil.

A detective investigates a series of gruesome murders,
only to discover they're all connected to a sinister cult.

Zombies roam the streets, hungry for flesh and blood.

Lurking in the darkness is a creature that
preys on the souls of the living.

You find a mysterious letter that reveals a
terrifying truth about your past.

Unholy rituals are performed in the abandoned church,
summoning dark spirits from the beyond.

Knocking on the door in the middle of the night,
no one expected who would answer.

A tribe of prehistoric humans is terrorized by a
race of intelligent dinosaurs who have become
the dominant species on the planet.

You hear a phone ringing in an empty room,
but there's no phone there.

The ticking of the clock became louder with each passing minute, until it was the only sound in the room. Suddenly, the clock face twisted into a grotesque, leering grin.

In a small village, a group of survivors must fight against a coven of witches that have taken over the town.

Panic spreads as an unknown virus begins to turn humans into flesh-eating monsters.

Crumbling gravestones reveal the presence of a malevolent spirit in the old cemetery.

The scent of rot and decay hung heavily in the air, as I stumbled upon an ancient burial ground. As I stepped closer, the corpses began to rise from their graves, their eyes fixed hungrily upon me.

Living in a Soviet country, you realize that even speaking out against the government can have dire consequences.

A small town is plagued by a series of strange weather patterns, and the only clue is a mysterious figure seen on the horizon.

Grotesque creatures lurk in the depths of the abandoned mine, waiting for their next prey.

Zoned out on the bus ride, they didn't realize they were heading towards an unknown destination.

In a world where everyone has a food allergy, a new company develops a pill that cures all allergies. But the pill has a horrifying side effect.

Just beyond the gates of the old cemetery, a dark figure watches, waiting to claim its next victim.

A group of time travelers go back to prehistoric
times and accidentally alter the timeline,
resulting in an apocalyptic future.

A family moves into a remote farmhouse, only to discover
it's haunted by the ghosts of its former inhabitants.

You find a strange portal in your closet
that leads to another world.

Ravenous beasts hunt in the abandoned zoo,
tearing apart anything in their path.

You hear a voice calling your name from inside a closet, but when you open it, no one's there.

68

A group of friends go on a camping trip, but soon realize that they've stumbled upon a sacrificial site.

Every night, I heard the sound of soft whispers coming from the empty closet. One night, I finally mustered the courage to investigate - only to find an ancient, decaying hand reaching out to grab me.

A group of survivors must navigate a world where the dead come back to life, but they soon realize that not all zombies are the same.

Deathly silence fills the abandoned prison,
but what lies within its walls?

In the forest, strange markings lead to a mysterious ritual site.

A tribe of prehistoric humans discovers an ancient underwater
civilization that has been dormant for millennia, but
disturbing its slumber awakens a terrible monster.

A group of college students go on a trip to a remote
cabin in the woods, only to find themselves hunted
by a group of cannibalistic hillbillies.

You wake up with a strange mark on your
forehead that won't go away.

The baker's bread was a staple in the small village, but
no one knew the recipe passed down from the previous
generations included something more sinister.

A group of humans on a research mission to a
distant star system discover a terrifying, sentient
form of energy that possesses their bodies.

A woman wakes up in a strange laboratory with
no memory of how she got there. The only food
available is a strange, glowing substance.

Hidden deep in the forest is an ancient temple,
guarded by an unseen force.

You see a ghostly figure in the reflection of a puddle of water.

A young couple moves into an old mansion, but they
soon realize that the house has a dark history.

Quaking with fear, a group of survivors hides from
the zombie horde in a deserted building.

You see a ghostly figure in the mirror that moves
independently of your own reflection.

You find a mysterious book with strange symbols
on the cover, and you can't resist opening it.

The last remaining religious leader is a machine, and it
demands obedience from all humans. How do they rebel?

You hear the sound of someone whispering
your name in the darkness.

In a galaxy where religious zealots rule, a team of scientists must uncover the truth about the origins of their society.

In a post-apocalyptic world, a cult leader's followers must decide whether to trust him or escape.

The butcher's meats were said to be the best in town, but no one dared to question the strange rituals that went on behind the shop's closed doors.

A crew on a mining vessel unearths a mysterious artifact that begins to manipulate their minds and actions.

A woman inherits an old book from her grandfather, but soon realizes that it's a grimoire with dangerous spells.

A group of survivors must navigate a world where the laws of magic are real and dangerous.

A woman starts experiencing strange occurrences in her home, and soon realizes that she's being haunted by a ghost.

Madness descends upon a small town after a mysterious meteor crashes nearby.

A woman starts experiencing strange dreams, and soon realizes that they're more than just dreams.

You hear a child crying in the darkness, but there's no one there when you investigate.

A woman starts experiencing strange dreams that seem to be connected to a mysterious ritual.

You see a strange, shadowy figure in the corner of your eye, but when you turn to look, it's gone.

A young woman is stalked by a mysterious figure, only to realize too late that it's a supernatural being with sinister intentions.

In a universe where gods are real, an atheist must find a way to survive.

In a future society, a corporation has developed a way to turn human waste into edible protein bars. But something about the process isn't quite right.

You wake up to find a strange plant growing in your room.

You wake up to find your house has been rearranged overnight.

As a man investigates a series of strange
occurrences in his town, he soon realizes that
they're all connected to a mysterious book.

In a small village in the middle of nowhere, a strange cult
holds a ritual that causes the dead to rise from their graves.

You see your doppelganger walking towards
you, but it's not a reflection.

Beneath the town lies an ancient burial
ground that holds a terrible secret.

The room suddenly fills with an unexplainable
coldness, and you can see your breath.

You hear the sound of a piano playing in an
empty room, but there's no piano.

Restless spirits haunt the halls of a hospital that
was built over a long-forgotten graveyard.

Yearning for revenge, the ghosts of the past
haunt the halls of an old mansion.

A group of friends visit a supposedly haunted amusement
park, but soon realize that the rides are not safe.

The children in town are acting strangely,
almost as if they're possessed.

A woman wakes up in a hospital, but she can't remember
how she got there or why she's covered in blood.

Yearning for vengeance, the restless dead rise from their graves.

After being exiled from his religious community, a man discovers a hidden society where religion is celebrated in secret.

The radio starts playing a song that you've never heard before, and it won't turn off.

A small town is plagued by a mysterious fog that seems to be infecting the residents.

In a post-apocalyptic world, a small community discovers that their robotic caretakers have turned against them.

A man starts experiencing strange time loops, and soon realizes that he's not the only one stuck in this never-ending day.

After a virus wipes out all religion on Earth, aliens arrive to bring back faith - but at what cost?

The antique shop had a strange collection of items that seemed to be cursed.

You find a strange, ancient artifact that seems to be alive.

You hear the sound of someone knocking on your front door in the middle of the night.

You hear the sound of someone tapping on your window, but there's no one there.

A food truck appears in a small town and quickly becomes popular. But the customers start disappearing.

An experimental spacecraft goes off course, leading its crew to a hostile, uncharted planet.

A group of friends explore a supposedly haunted mansion, but soon realize that the ghosts are not friendly.

I woke up in the middle of the night to find a stranger sitting at the foot of my bed, watching me sleep. As he got up to leave, he left behind a cold, lifeless handprint on my foot.

A woman moves into a new house, but soon realizes that the previous owners left something behind that's determined to kill her.

You wake up to find yourself in a different
house, with no explanation.

The crew of a space mission discovers an abandoned
ship filled with seemingly endless food supplies. But
they soon realize the food has a sinister origin.

An astronaut on a solo mission discovers a
mysterious signal coming from an abandoned
planetoid, leading to a horrifying discovery.

Haunted by the past, the old asylum holds a secret
that threatens to destroy all who enter.

The old book I found in the attic was filled with strange symbols and incantations. As I read them aloud, I felt a sharp pain in my chest, and watched in horror as a pair of twisted, demonic wings burst from my back.

Quivering with fear, a young couple investigates the abandoned farmhouse.

A woman starts experiencing strange and terrifying hallucinations after eating a mysterious fruit.

A man invents a machine that can replicate any food. But the machine has a terrifying ability to bring back long-dead ingredients.

A group of humans on a colonization mission to
a distant planet find themselves being hunted
by a ruthless, extraterrestrial predator.

The old book in the library is bound in human
skin, and it's waiting to be opened.

A woman inherits an old mansion from her deceased uncle,
only to discover it's haunted by his vengeful spirit.

Glimpses of a dark figure can be seen in the
abandoned mansion's windows at night.

When the lights went out, they knew they
were not alone in the house.

A group of survivors must navigate a world where the sun
never sets, and the darkness holds unspeakable horrors.

The darkness under your bed hides more than just dust bunnies.

A group of survivors must fight against an army
of possessed dolls that have come to life.

The food truck's tacos were the talk of the town, but customers
who ordered the "special" menu item never returned.

Wandering through the mist, a lost traveler
stumbles upon a cursed village.

A man starts seeing strange visions of a demon, and
soon realizes that it's trying to possess him.

You hear a child's laughter in the darkness,
but there's no child around.

A group of friends visit a supposedly abandoned asylum, but soon realize that they're not alone.

Wandering through the woods, a lost traveler stumbles upon a group of witches performing a ritual.

A group of friends explore an abandoned hospital, but soon realize that they've stumbled upon a secret experiment gone wrong.

A group of astronauts on a mission to colonize a new planet discovers a mysterious food source. But it has a terrifying effect on their bodies and minds.

On a remote asteroid, a group of humans discover a horrifying, ancient creature that has been locked away for eons.

A newly discovered cave painting tells the story of a tribe of prehistoric humans who were haunted by a monstrous creature in the night.

In a future where religion is considered a mental illness, a man must hide his beliefs or risk being institutionalized.

You wake up to find your room covered in a thick layer of fog.

You find a strange, antique mirror at a garage sale,
but every reflection shows someone else's face.

On a remote planetoid, a scientific experiment
with alien technology goes wrong, leading to a
terrifying transformation of the researchers.

The barbeque pitmaster's sauce was legendary, but no one
knew that it was made with the blood of his enemies.

You hear the sound of a child's laughter
coming from an empty room.

In the darkness of the forest, they found a
tree with a strange mark on it.

Don't answer the phone after dark, it's always the dead calling.

The walls of the abandoned hospital were covered in blood
and graffiti, as I made my way to the top floor. There, I
found a group of doctors performing surgeries on each
other, their screams echoing through the halls.

You find a cursed object that seems to bring
bad luck to everyone who touches it.

A cursed forest consumes those who enter,
trapping them forever in its depths.

Shadows dance in the moonlight, revealing the
presence of a supernatural entity.

The darkness in the basement has a life of its own.

Restless spirits haunt the old graveyard,
seeking revenge on the living.

X-ray vision reveals a twisted and deformed
skeleton, a result of a cruel experiment.

94

Xylophone music filled the air, but there was no one playing it.

Rummaging through the attic, they found
an old, mysterious book.

A woman starts experiencing strange changes in her memories,
and soon realizes that she's not the only one who's affected.

Creepy dolls in a small town antique shop come to life at night and start wreaking havoc on the unsuspecting residents.

A strange illness spreads through a small community, turning people into something monstrous.

You find a box of old photos that show disturbing images you don't remember.

You wake up to find yourself in a different time period, with no way back.

Fear consumes the small town as a mysterious
illness spreads, causing madness and death.

A mysterious object falls from the sky, and strange
things start happening to those who touch it.

You wake up in a strange, dark room, and the
door is locked from the outside.

In a small town, a series of unexplained
disappearances has everyone on edge.

People started disappearing after the strange comet appeared in the sky.

A small community is terrorized by a creature that only comes out at night, but the residents soon realize that it's not from this world.

A team of scientists on a research mission to study an alien planet discovers that the planet itself is alive and hostile.

A man discovers a secret door in his basement, but soon realizes that the things behind it should have stayed hidden.

After discovering a long-lost holy book, a man must decide
whether to share its contents with the world or keep it a secret.

A woman starts seeing strange figures in the shadows,
but when she turns on the light, they disappear.

From the depths of the ocean comes a creature
beyond human comprehension.

Living in Soviet Russia, you learn that the
government isn't the only thing to fear.

A man starts experiencing strange sensations in his body, and soon realizes that he's being possessed by a demon.

Underneath the city, an underground cult performed unspeakable rituals.

Living in a Soviet country, you're taught from a young age to never question authority.

The dolls in the antique shop seem to be watching you, and they're not friendly.

A space station crew receives a shipment of food
from a distant planet. But they soon realize the
food is alive and has taken over the ship.

Paranormal activity escalates in the abandoned hotel, but why?

You see a ghostly figure standing in the
middle of a deserted road.

The canned goods on the grocery store shelves were
contaminated with a virus that spread like wildfire.

Ghostly apparitions appear in a small, rural church, leaving the congregation petrified with fear.

A small town is plagued by a series of unexplainable fires, and the only clue is a strange odor left behind.

A woman starts seeing strange symbols everywhere she goes, and soon realizes that they're part of a demonic language.

You see a ghostly figure in the mirror, but it's not your reflection.

The street vendor's savory pies were a hit with the locals, but no one could identify the meat filling.

Laughter echoed through the abandoned carnival, but no one was there to make it.

Jarring events lead to the unearthing of dark secrets in a seemingly normal suburban neighborhood.

The brilliant scientist who defected to the United States starts to experience terrifying hallucinations that seem to be linked to the secrets he brought with him.

You find a secret room in your basement that reveals a dark past.

Hidden in the attic is a diary that reveals the
dark history of the old mansion.

When the family moved into their new home, they
discovered a mysterious root cellar filled with jars of
pickled vegetables that were anything but ordinary.

Foul odors emanate from the abandoned hospital,
signaling the presence of something evil.

A new cooking show features a chef who claims to have found a way to cook food from alternate universes. But the more the audience watches, the more they realize something isn't right.

The sound of a lullaby echoes through the empty house, but you're home alone.

You find a mysterious note that seems to predict your every move.

You hear scratching sounds coming from inside the walls, but there's no way in.

On a planet where the atmosphere is toxic to humans, a small community discovers a dangerous, mind-controlling parasite that threatens to consume them all.

Zombified soldiers rise from the dead, seeking revenge on those who betrayed them.

In a society where religion is a form of currency, a man must decide whether to trade his faith for wealth and power.

A woman starts experiencing strange weather phenomena whenever she gets angry.

In the abandoned house, you hear footsteps
coming up the stairs.

A team of explorers on a deep space mission discovers a
horrifying, cosmic entity that threatens to destroy them all.

A young woman must navigate a world where religion
and science are at odds with each other.

A group of explorers discovers a planet where
religion is a living, breathing entity.

A man discovers a strange artifact in an ancient temple, but soon realizes that it has the power to bring back the dead.

An alien race arrives on Earth and begins to experiment on prehistoric humans, resulting in monstrous hybrids that threaten to destroy the planet.

I walked through the abandoned city, my footsteps echoing through the empty streets. Suddenly, I heard the sound of a child's laughter, followed by a pair of glowing eyes staring at me from the darkness.

A man buys an antique mirror at an estate sale, only to discover it shows him a sinister reflection.

A group of explorers discover an ancient tomb,
but they soon realize they were not alone.

Lost in the catacombs beneath the city, a group of
tourists discover a horrifying truth about its past.

A woman starts experiencing strange changes
in her appearance, and soon realizes that she's
turning into something inhuman.

You hear the sound of something crawling on the
ceiling, but when you look up, nothing's there.

In a society where artificial intelligence has taken over, a group of humans must navigate a dangerous virtual reality world to survive.

You feel like someone is watching you, even though you're alone in the room.

A group of dissidents who dig a tunnel under the Berlin Wall discover that the ground they are excavating is cursed, leading to a series of terrifying encounters.

A group of survivors must navigate a post-apocalyptic world filled with danger and uncertainty.

Otherworldly entities have begun to invade our
world, bringing with them untold terror.

A group of survivors in a post-apocalyptic world
discover that prehistoric creatures have survived and
are now the dominant species on the planet.

Yearning for revenge, a vengeful spirit haunts the
halls of an old prison, tormenting the guards.

In a world where people are born with supernatural abilities,
those without powers are seen as second-class citizens.

A young couple moves into a charming old
house, only to discover its dark history and the
sinister forces that reside within.

The all-you-can-eat buffet seemed like a bargain, but the
food left a strange aftertaste that lingered for days.

The diner's signature dish was a breakfast sandwich, but the
eggs were always overcooked and had a strange green tint.

The small-town café had a cult following for their famous
chili, but it was rumored to be made with human remains.

You see a strange figure standing in the
middle of an empty field.

A small village is terrorized by a creature
that only comes out at night.

The cursed painting on the wall changes
every time you look at it.

You wake up to find yourself trapped in
a never-ending nightmare.

A group of astronauts land on a distant planet and discover that prehistoric humans still exist and are being hunted by a terrifying alien species.

An alien species that feeds on human emotion has infiltrated a fast food chain, causing patrons to experience extreme emotions while eating.

The abandoned carnival still has the screams of the trapped performers.

Visions of a dark future haunt the dreams of those who venture into the abandoned laboratory.

You find a mysterious key that unlocks a
door to another dimension.

A woman starts experiencing strange glitches in reality,
and soon realizes that she's trapped in a simulation.

In a future where the universe is ruled by a theocratic
government, a group of rebels must overthrow the regime.

Up in the mountains, they stumbled upon
an ancient burial ground.

The abandoned factory still echoes with
the screams of the workers.

Mangled bodies litter the streets of the abandoned
city, a gruesome reminder of the apocalypse.

Ghostly apparitions haunt the halls of the abandoned hospital.

A group of friends explore an old mine, but soon
realize that they're not alone underground.

A family moves into a new house, but strange things start to happen, and they soon realize that the house has a dark past.

Desperate for answers, a group of investigators delves into the mysteries of the occult.

Rumors of a cursed object had circulated for generations, until someone found it.

Rattling chains and creaking floorboards signal the presence of a malevolent ghost.

A woman starts to have vivid nightmares
that seem to be coming true.

The shadows on the wall take on a life of their own at night.

A woman must find a way to reconcile her faith with
the scientific evidence that contradicts it.

As a woman starts experiencing strange changes in her
body, she soon realizes that she's not entirely human.

You smell something rotting, but you can't find the source.

A man starts experiencing strange visions of a dark future, and soon realizes that he has the power to change it.

You find a hidden room in your house that contains something sinister.

In the attic, a cursed mirror reflects a sinister presence.

Obsessed with immortality, a mad scientist
creates an army of the undead.

A woman moves into a new apartment, but soon realizes
that her neighbors are not what they seem.

A woman inherits an old family curse that causes her
to transform into a werewolf under the full moon.

A man starts to suspect that his wife may
not be who she appears to be.

In a society where human cloning is common, a clone begins
to experience terrifying glitches in their genetic code.

Midnight screams can be heard coming from
the old mansion on the hill.

A young couple moves into a new apartment, only to
discover it's built on the site of an ancient burial ground.

You find a hidden passage in your house that
leads to a terrifying discovery.

Zigzagging through the dark alley, they felt
a presence following them.

Year after year, the same gruesome murder
occurred on the same day.

You wake up to find a strange symbol etched into your flesh.

A woman inherits a house from a distant relative, but
soon discovers that the house has a dark past.

The small bakery in the countryside was famous
for their pies, but no one knew that the filling was
made from the flesh of the townsfolk.

You find a strange creature in your backyard
that shouldn't exist in this world.

The old abandoned hospital on the edge of town has
been reopened, but the patients never seem to leave.

You see a ghostly figure in the reflection of a dark window.

In a world where cybernetic implants have become the norm, a group of humans discovers a sinister conspiracy to control their minds through their implants.

The shadow of a person passes by your window, but when you look outside, no one is there.

A man discovers a portal to another dimension, but soon realizes that the creatures on the other side are not friendly.

A woman starts receiving strange phone calls from an unknown number, but when she answers, there's no one there.

The town's annual chili cook-off was a fierce competition, but rumors circulated about a secret ingredient that no one dared to ask about.

Shadows moved on their own in the abandoned hospital, but there was no wind.

In a society where technology is used to enforce religious beliefs, a hacker must find a way to break free.

Night falls, and the haunted forest comes alive with malevolent spirits and creatures.

Only the bravest souls dare to explore the abandoned mine, where unspeakable horrors await.

You see a ghostly apparition in a mirror that isn't there when you turn around.

Driven mad by the whispers, they begged for the voices to stop.

Flickering lights reveal the presence of a malevolent ghost in the old lighthouse.

You see a ghostly figure in your dreams that
seems to be trying to warn you.

A spaceship crew discovers a planet where the
inhabitants worship an unknown entity - but the
entity may be closer than they think.

A group of teenagers go on a camping trip, but they
soon realize that they're not alone in the woods.

A man wakes up in an unfamiliar hotel room
with no memory of how he got there, only to
discover he's trapped in a sinister game.

A new restaurant opens that serves food made entirely from lab-grown meat. But the staff quickly realize that the meat is taking on a life of its own.

A young woman inherits an old house from her grandmother, only to discover it's haunted by the ghosts of her ancestors.

A small community is terrorized by a mysterious creature that seems to be made of metal.

A group of friends play a game that summons a malevolent spirit, only to realize they've unleashed something far more powerful than they ever imagined.

Echoes of the past can be heard in the abandoned
theater, where a tragic event occurred.

The crypt in the cemetery holds secrets that
are better left undiscovered.

In a future where religion is strictly enforced, a group of
rebels must find a way to escape to a distant planet.

The eerie glow of the abandoned laboratory signals
a dangerous experiment gone wrong.

Beneath the icy surface of a distant moon, a research team discovers a horrifying, ancient civilization.

You find a strange object that seems to be growing in size.

Beyond the mist lies a world of nightmares that few have ever seen.

As a man investigates a series of strange disappearances in his town, he soon realizes that the culprit is something not of this world.

You wake up in a hospital room, surrounded by
doctors with strange, inhuman eyes.

The new chocolate factory promised an unforgettable
taste experience, but the workers who disappeared
during the night shift were never seen again.

You wake up to find yourself in a different
body, with no explanation.

A group of friends decide to explore a supposedly
abandoned mansion, but they soon realize that
something is waiting for them inside.

As a group of friends go on a road trip, they soon realize that the roads are not what they seem, and that they're trapped in a never-ending loop.

A group of survivors band together after a catastrophic event, but soon realize that their greatest enemy might be each other.

A group of survivors must navigate a world where technology has turned against them.

A scientific experiment gone wrong results in a group of humans gaining dangerous telekinetic abilities.

In the abandoned mine, the dead miners still haunt the tunnels.

A genetically modified plant is found on a distant planet that can sustain life. But the crew that brought it back to Earth soon realize the plant is taking over their bodies.

You smell something burning, but the smoke is coming from under the floorboards.

A group of friends find an old Ouija board and decide to use it for fun, but they accidentally summon something evil.

The mirror shows you a glimpse of a different reality where everything is wrong.

You wake up to find yourself in a different dimension, with no way back.

The car you're driving takes you to a place you don't recognize, and it won't let you leave.

The walls of my house started to shift and warp, the ground beneath my feet tilting at a sickening angle. Suddenly, I was standing on the edge of a cliff, staring down into an endless abyss.

An experiment to clone a prehistoric man goes
awry when the creature is brought back to life and
proves to be an unstoppable killing machine.

Ghostly whispers can be heard in the abandoned
asylum, but the patients are long gone.

You hear the sound of someone laughing in the darkness.

Chaos erupts when a strange virus turns
people into savage beasts.

You thought it was just a game until the players
started disappearing one by one.

In the shadows of the abandoned factory,
something stirs, hungry for blood.

A group of humans on a space station encounter a dangerous,
reality-bending anomaly that threatens to tear them apart.

You hear the sound of a woman singing
a lullaby in the darkness.

A woman discovers that the religious leaders who raised her were actually aliens studying human belief systems.

You find a mysterious book that seems to be written in an unknown language.

The house on the hill holds secrets that will never be uncovered.

In a world where technology has become sentient, a group of survivors must fight against machines that have turned against their creators.

Gathering around the campfire, they shared
ghost stories that turned out to be true.

Paranormal activity intensifies in the old library,
as the ghosts of past readers refuse to leave.

In the sewers, a mutated monster preys on
unsuspecting victims who wander too close.

A woman starts experiencing strange visions
of a demonic figure, and soon realizes that it's
trying to communicate with her.

A man wakes up in a strange room with no memory of
how he got there, and soon realizes that he's not alone.

A tribe of prehistoric humans discovers an ancient spacecraft
buried deep in the earth, but their curiosity unleashes a
malevolent alien presence that threatens to destroy them all.

You see a ghostly apparition in your room that
seems to be trying to communicate with you.

X-rays reveal a horrifying mutation in the
genetic makeup of a small community.

Hidden in the shadows is a creature that feeds on human fear.

A scientist develops a pill that eliminates the need for food altogether. But it comes with a horrifying side effect.

The caterer's hors d'oeuvres were sophisticated, but the secret ingredient was something that could not be found on any grocery store shelf.

Kinetic energy builds in the abandoned power plant, signaling a dangerous explosion.

You find a mysterious journal that seems to
contain the secrets of the universe.

The old house you just moved into has a room that's always
locked, and you can hear something moving inside.

You wake up with a strange mark on your
arm that you can't explain.

Quiet whispers filled the old library, but
there was no one around.

A mysterious force begins to possess the minds
of a group of humans on a distant colony,
turning them into savage monsters.

Poisonous spores fill the air, leading to a mass hallucination.

A man starts experiencing strange time loops, and soon
realizes that he's trapped in a never-ending nightmare.

Unearthly screams echo through the abandoned
factory, but who – or what – is making them?

You see a strange light in the sky that seems to be following you.

The antique doll you inherited from your grandmother moves on its own, and it's not a gentle gesture.

A medical experiment gone wrong leads to a group of humans developing deadly, supernatural abilities.

In a world where technology is implanted into the human body, a virus begins to infect the implants, turning people into uncontrollable machines.

Nightmarish apparitions haunt the dreams of those
who explore the abandoned theme park.

A man starts experiencing strange time skips, and soon
realizes that he's living the same day over and over again.

You hear the sound of a choir singing in an abandoned church.

You find a strange book in a library that
reveals a world of horrors.

The food critic was invited to a private tasting, but the menu consisted of exotic meats that were too bizarre to be identified.

A group of explorers stumble upon a hidden prehistoric civilization that has evolved to possess psychic abilities and use them to terrorize outsiders.

A prehistoric virus is released from a melting glacier and infects the crew of a research station, turning them into ravenous monsters.

You find a cursed doll that seems to move on its own.

You wake up to find yourself in a hospital bed,
with no memory of how you got there.

You hear the sound of scratching coming from inside the walls.

A tribe of prehistoric humans begin to worship a
strange glowing orb, which turns out to be a gateway
to another dimension full of unspeakable horrors.

A woman is haunted by a demon that possesses her
dreams, driving her to the brink of insanity.

A scientist conducts an experiment to bring the dead back
to life, but the results are far from what he expected.

The trees in the forest start to move, and
they're not supposed to.

You wake up to find yourself buried alive in a coffin.

A group of friends go on a road trip, but soon realize that
they've entered a town that doesn't exist on any map.

The pancake house's maple syrup was a hit with the customers, but no one knew that it was infused with a voodoo curse.

A food corporation creates a genetically modified plant that can grow in any environment. But the plant has a terrifying defense mechanism.

A young girl discovers that she has the power to communicate with the dead, but this ability comes at a terrible cost.

Monsters roam the streets at night, but they're not what you think they are.

No one knows what happened to the missing
hikers on the mountain.

A team of scientists travel back in time to study prehistoric
humans, but they accidentally bring back a deadly
disease that threatens to wipe out humanity.

You find a strange key that unlocks a door to a world of horrors.

In a world where nightmares can come to life, a group
of survivors must fight against their worst fears.

A tribe of prehistoric humans develop the ability to control and manipulate the elements, leading to devastating consequences.

After a near-death experience, a man discovers that he has the power to see through the illusions of religion.

Zoological anomalies run rampant in an abandoned research facility, but what created them?

The smell of gasoline filled the air as I walked down the deserted street, the abandoned cars eerily silent. Then, a faint humming started, growing louder until a giant, sentient machine rose up from the shadows.

After a cataclysmic event destroys civilization, a group of survivors forms a new religion based on their experiences.

A fast food chain introduces a new burger that can induce vivid dreams. But the dreams turn into nightmares.

A prehistoric virus is released from deep within the earth, causing humans to mutate into horrifying creatures with uncontrollable appetites.

Witches gather in the abandoned cabin, preparing to unleash a dark ritual on the world.

Jolts of electricity reveal a shocking secret
hidden in the basement laboratory.

The winery's vintage bottles were highly sought
after, but the grapes were grown in soil that
was cursed by the spirits of the land.

After being exposed to a dangerous alien substance, a group
of humans begin to experience terrifying mutations.

In a society where artificial intelligence has become
self-aware, a group of humans must fight for their
survival against their own creations.

Strange occurrences begin to happen in a small
town after the arrival of a new family.

The woods are quiet, too quiet, and the only sound
you hear is your own heart beating.

You see a mysterious figure standing at
the end of a long hallway.

A group of hikers gets lost in the woods, but they
soon realize something is hunting them.

A cursed object brings death and destruction
to all who possess it.

You see strange symbols etched into your skin
that you don't remember getting.

You hear the sound of someone crying in the
darkness, but there's no one there.

In a post-apocalyptic world, a group of survivors must fend
off not only zombies, but also a new kind of monster.

Every night, I heard a soft humming coming from the walls of my bedroom. One night, I finally decided to investigate, only to find a portal to a world made entirely of flesh and bone.

Vacations are supposed to be relaxing, but not in this haunted hotel.

A woman inherits a cursed doll from her grandmother, but soon realizes that the doll has a mind of its own.

Terror grips a group of travelers stranded in the middle of the ocean on a seemingly abandoned ship.

Unearthly screams fill the night air as a vengeful spirit seeks revenge on its killers.

You see a ghostly figure standing in the doorway of an empty room.

A mad scientist creates a machine that can turn any inanimate object into edible food. But the machine has a twisted sense of humor.

The fresh seafood market was a popular attraction, but the fisherman who caught the fish disappeared one by one.

You find a mysterious box that seems to be alive.

A family moves into a new house, but the
previous owner never really left.

Terrifying dreams haunt the mind of a survivor
who escaped the clutches of a mad scientist.

A child's imaginary friend starts to show up in
your dreams, and it's not friendly anymore.

You see a figure standing in your yard that looks like a person but isn't quite human.

In a society where robots have replaced human workers, a group of rogue robots begin to take on a dangerous, sentient intelligence.

A scientist discovers a way to resurrect prehistoric animals, but their DNA has been contaminated and they are now deadly monsters.

Horror strikes a small group of friends who find themselves stranded in a remote cabin in the woods.

Underneath the floorboards, something stirs in the darkness.

A team of astronauts travel to a distant planet and find that prehistoric creatures have evolved into intelligent beings who are now seeking revenge on humanity.

A mining colony on a remote asteroid discovers a dangerous, shape-shifting creature that infiltrates their ranks.

You hear the sound of someone whispering
in your ear when you're alone.

A group of survivors must navigate a world where time is not a constant, and reality itself is constantly shifting.

You hear footsteps coming up the stairs, but there's no one there when you look.

You see a strange figure in the woods that disappears when you try to approach it.

Strange occurrences plague the small town, pointing to an otherworldly presence.

A mysterious fog descends on a small town, bringing
with it a horde of ravenous creatures.

A sentient alien species offers Earth a cure for world
hunger in exchange for a terrifying trade-off.

You find a diary in your attic that reveals a dark family secret.

You receive an anonymous message that
predicts your every move.

You see a mysterious figure watching you from across the street.

The rebel group that takes to the forests soon discovers
that they are not alone - there are creatures in the woods
that are even more dangerous than the Soviet patrols.

The new neighbors in town were not what they seemed.

You find a cursed object in your possession
that you can't get rid of.

Candles flickered in the abandoned church,
but no one had lit them.

Lurking in the shadows is a creature that hunts by night.

In the future, a lab-grown protein becomes the only
food source. But it comes at a horrifying cost.

The forest has eyes that follow you, waiting
for the perfect moment to strike.

In a small town, a group of survivors must navigate a world where the laws of physics no longer apply.

The door creaks open on its own, revealing a pitch-black room beyond.

A man inherits an old house from his grandfather, but soon realizes that the house is cursed and that it's haunted by vengeful spirits.

In a universe where a god-like being controls all life, a group of rebels must overthrow the entity to regain their freedom.

A group of friends stumble upon a strange cave system, but soon realize that it's a portal to another dimension.

A man starts experiencing strange phenomena in his dreams, and soon realizes that he's being haunted by a vengeful spirit.

In the abandoned town, the dead still walk the streets.

You see a figure in your peripheral vision that disappears when you turn to look.

You see someone standing outside your window,
but they're floating six feet above the ground.

A group of friends stumble upon an abandoned
carnival, but it's not as empty as it seems.

Nightmares become reality as a shadowy
figure stalks the streets.

You hear the sound of a baby crying in the
distance, but it's getting louder.

A group of strangers are forced to participate in a deadly game where the stakes are life and death.

A small town is plagued by a series of unexplainable power outages, and the only clue is a strange humming sound.

After a catastrophic event on Earth, the remaining humans survive on rationed space food. But it's not long before they realize the food is changing them.

As the moon rises, a pack of werewolves emerges from the shadows to hunt.

Yearning for freedom, the captive spirits of an old prison seek revenge on their captors.

Living in a Soviet country, you learn to distrust even your closest friends and family.

The old photograph album you found in the attic shows pictures of people who never existed.

Fog rolls in, bringing with it strange and unsettling creatures that have never been seen before.

You hear the sound of a woman weeping in
the night, but you can't find her.

A woman moves into a new apartment, but soon realizes
that the previous tenant left something behind.

Moonlit shadows reveal the presence of a terrifying
creature in the abandoned warehouse.

The sound of dripping water echoed through the
deserted subway tunnel, as I followed the trail of
blood to a figure crouched in the shadows. It turned to
face me, revealing a face made entirely of eyes.

A strange cult moves into a small town, and
the residents start acting strangely.

You see a mysterious figure standing
outside your window at night.

You find a mysterious painting that seems to be cursed.

A group of astronauts on a colonization mission
to a distant planet discover a horrifying, ancient
temple that holds a sinister secret.

Just beyond the veil of reality lies a realm of pure terror.

A man starts experiencing bizarre and disturbing
hallucinations after eating a mysterious substance.

Everyone told her not to go in the basement,
but she didn't listen.

You wake up to find a stranger sleeping in
your bed, but they're not human.

The lighthouse on the shore guides the lost to their doom.

Dark magic holds the key to defeating the evil
that lurks in the abandoned church.

You hear the sound of an infant crying,
but you don't have a baby.

Just when they thought they were safe, they
heard the scratching at the door.

You find a trapdoor in the basement, and it leads
to a tunnel you've never seen before.

You hear the sound of footsteps in your
house when you're home alone.

A group of friends stumble upon a mysterious creature in
the woods, but soon realize that it's not from this world.

A couple moves into a new apartment, but strange
things start to happen when they go to sleep.

You wake up to find a mysterious symbol
drawn on your bedroom floor.

In a world where people are born with supernatural
abilities, a dangerous cult arises, seeking to harness
these powers for their own purposes.

The old well in the backyard seems to be calling to you.

You see a ghostly figure at the end of the hallway,
but it disappears when you approach it.

You wake up to find a strange smell coming from your closet.

The sushi chef's knives moved with precision, but
the fish he used came from a toxic source.

When the clock strikes midnight, the walls begin to whisper.

A group of friends stumble upon a strange book that seems to be
written in an unknown language, but when they start reading
it, they realize they are casting a spell that can't be undone.

A group of archeologists uncover a prehistoric
virus that has been dormant for millions of years,
and it soon infects the entire world.

A group of friends go on a hike, but soon realize
that the forest is not what it seems.

Blood stains the walls of the abandoned hospital, a
testament to the horrors that occurred within.

A man inherits a farm that grows a strange crop that seems
to move on its own. But the crop has a deadly secret.

A small community is terrorized by a creature
that seems to be made of fire.

Nightmarish visions plague the minds of those who
dare to enter the abandoned laboratory.

You hear a voice whispering your name from an old photograph.

You wake up in a strange place with no
memory of how you got there.

A group of explorers venture into an uncharted cave system, only to discover they're not alone underground.

Nightmares become reality as a mysterious force possesses the residents of a small, coastal town.

A malfunction in a terraforming system on a distant planet creates deadly, mutated creatures.

In a world where the dead can be brought back to life, a group of survivors must fight against a new plague that causes the dead to become unstoppable.

Voices from beyond the grave warned them
of the impending danger.

A woman discovers a mysterious package on her
doorstep, but soon realizes that it's a cursed object.

You wake up to find a strange person standing over you,
but they disappear when you try to touch them.

After a spaceship crash-lands on a distant planet, the crew
must navigate a world ruled by a fanatical religious order.

In a future world where humans have developed the ability to teleport, a deadly virus begins to spread through the teleportation network.

Crawling through the darkness, a survivor desperately tries to escape the zombie horde.

A woman starts experiencing strange changes in her personality, and soon realizes that she cannot control herself during certain hours of the day.

Memories of the past haunted them as they revisited their childhood home.